STARTING A CHILDCARE BUSINESS WITHOUT A LOAN

By

Natalie Moore

This book is dedicated to my children. They are the reason, I continue to push forward in my career. My children are my legacy, my foundation. I also dedicate this book to all upcoming Childcare Bosses who are looking to make their dreams come true.

Remember in a world filled with Bosses. ….
Be a Mogul.

Natalie Moore

Steps to Success

The Step to Entrepreneurship

Live daringly, boldly, fearlessly. Taste the relish to be found in competition – in having put forth the best within you. ~ Henry J. Kaiser

You've made the wonderful decision to start your own daycare center. The commitment of providing quality daycare to families in your community is rewarding and accompanies arduous work. It is important that you begin this journey with an effective business plan. It is essential to be well educated on the start-up and operating costs of your center. This will assure success in your business and create the foundation for operational growth. *Entrepreneur,* a magazine and online resource for business owners, cites that startup costs average between $10,000 and $50,000. However, there is a simple and less costly way of achieving these figures. The concept of facilitating the opening of your daycare center without a loan is contributory to your economic success.

1

This is what I call "creative funding". It propels your opportunity for profits instead of a financial institution when initiating a loan. When starting my business, I was turned down by several financial institutions to whom I previously held long lasting business relationships with. This is when I decided to become creative and bold in my business. I knew that despite their no, God had said yes.

In my book, *Childcare Chronicles*, I mentioned when initially starting my center I implemented a business plan that was based on concrete economical strategies that saved me thousands of dollars. Negotiation can be beneficial in manifesting success with contractors and landlords. It is important to trust the process and alleviate haste in bringing the creation of your center to fruition. From the acquiring of business space to classroom supplies, the art of negotiation is imperative in the opening of your center. Negotiation is a part of our everyday lives, however it is a crucial component to your business success. It is important to have a strategy in place in order to gain a win for your business. If there is an amount that requires an amount that may not be in your budget, inquire if there is availability for payment arrangements. If this can be agreed upon, be consistent and honor your agreement. Good business relationships are what keep your doors open. Be honorable with your word and keep a clear and open line of communication with those you are in business with. You want to build a business Network that is comprised of vendors that benefit your business. These are business owners who you can form long lasting relationships with that can assist in the needs of your business. You never want to "burn your bridges" or compromise your integrity with those you do business. In addition to negotiation, the art of nurturing your business network is a huge component to you being a successful center owner. Do not shy away from being creative in your business. This is the time when your use of creativity can birth a win-win in opening your business.

Bargain, Bargain, Bargain

The person who does not ask will never get a bargain.
~ French Proverb

When you are building a business, it is important that you adopt an eye for quality but at a discounted price. Compulsive spending and purchasing without planning for your business can be detrimental to your start up budget. It is important to be open and creative when acquiring any items for your business. When starting your business, it is important to be as frugal as possible. Adopting an eye for things of quality at a lower cost is a definite asset to your overall business plan. Many business owners have confided to me that they have difficulty in this area. This is a skill that can be mastered through the appropriate training and coaching. If this is something that you need assistance with I offer services through my consulting service, Childcare Boss Marketing. I can provide a plan that will assist you with gaining the expertise and eye to this concept.

Craigslist and eBay

Many people fail to utilize both online outlets, Craigslist and eBay. This has been a Childcare Center goldmine for me. Craigslist, as well as eBay, has provided an opportunity for me to gain extraordinary supplies and furniture for my centers. Craigslist and eBay provide local contacts that are seeking to sell materials and items. Some daycares may be moving or going out of business and are looking for someone to purchase their items. This is when you must implement your negotiation skills with the sellers that you are meeting with. I have also been open to sellers that were outside my city as well. If the items are quality and fair price and worth the drive, then it is beneficial to take advantage of the opportunity.

Dollar Tree

Do you have a local Dollar Tree or Discount Dollar in your area? You can gain incredible manipulatives and teaching aids at both retail stores. Building a solid and quality curriculum can be achieved using many of the workbooks that are available for toddlers and preschoolers at these stores. The dynamic thing is that the ability to photocopy these items can assist in creating recyclable aids that you can use throughout the year.

School Districts

Have you created a relationship with School administration in your local area? I highly encourage you to create a relationship with School District officials. At the end of the year, many districts dispose of supplies and furniture because of the distribution of new materials. Why not take advantage of this opportunity? Do not be afraid to communicate your interest in the items available. This is an opportunity to gain quality materials at no cost. A definite plus for your business.

Garage Sales/Flea Markets

Do you know that you can find some hidden treasures at local garage sales and flea markets? Check your local newspaper outlet and websites for those upcoming garage sales and flea market opportunities. Facebook also has groups that are targeted towards garage sales and flea markets that are in your local area. Query your local area and garage sales or flea markets to gain information on your local area.

Commercial Rent

Bargain shopping comes in handy when negotiating your rent for your facility. There are plenty of ways that you can negotiate to gain a deferment for rent when your facility is under construction. I negotiated rent while under construction and did not begin to pay rent until the project was complete. My construction was between 8-9 months so during that time I did not pay one dime. I have negotiated this concept with all locations I own.

Playground Equipment

The playground equipment for your facility can be expensive. I have found that the best way to f facilitate this cost is to lease the equipment through a company or vendor. You may wonder why? First, it helps you to avoid presenting an exuberant amount of money to purchase the equipment with no insurance or repair policy on the equipment. Instead, when you lease the equipment you can implement the amount into your monthly expenditures and you can have guaranteed covered repair when you have an issue with the equipment. This eliminates pricey repair costs and it is overall a positive business move for your facility.

Transportation

An excellent perk of your business would be the implementation of transportation for students within your facility and those children that participate in after school activities. An average 15 passenger commercial van is about 30 k for a used vehicle. I have found that it is easier to lease to own these vehicles and pay them off within a 2-3-year period. This assures again that you are not overextending your outcome expenditures but creating a plan that will allow you room to grow.

Partnerships

One of the most lucrative ways to acquire facilities for prospective centers is through partnership. I have found many business owners who were shut down by licensing that were willing to negotiate the trading of their business, inclusive of clients, furniture, and materials. I have also participated in this type of transaction for my centers. This is a win-win for the prospective business owner because you find a center that is already zoned for childcare and you acquire a "ready-to-go" business to operate. One important fact that I recommend is that you negotiate with the owner to allow you deferments on rent for three months while you prepare the facility for licensing. It is important to assure that all bills and employee payroll has been fulfilled before taking over ownership of the lease.

When building your business and purchasing items, it is essential that you incorporate a sound purchasing plan. This will allow you financial control and alleviate an overwhelming overhead in your business.

Business to Business

A business that makes nothing but money is a poor business. ~ Henry Ford

Are you acquainted with the business owner who has an office across the street from your center? Do you know the name of the business owner that you may see daily? If your answer is no, this is a major oversight in your business.

It is very important that you extend yourself in networking with your fellow business neighbors so that they know who you are and create a word of mouth regarding your business. It is awesome to gain business online, but we must not forget to orchestrate business offline as well. As business owners operating in the same city, we face similar issues.

From city and road closures, rent and taxes, business owners have a huge voice in what occurs in their own communities. When owners can come together on the issues that affect them all, regardless of the industry, we all win. I've learned that networking within your business community can also create a phenomenal network and resource directory.

Business owners, through trial and error, have experienced failures and triumphs and can oftentimes offer advice and help in areas you are in question of. As business owners, we can assist each other in success.

Let's face it ... you opened a business to make money. But many small businesses close each year due to the struggle of getting people in the door. Marketing is a huge part of business success, and working together with your neighboring businesses can be a great tool in bringing people in the door. From cross-promotions to coordinating neighborhood events to strategic discounting, partnering with your neighbors can be a funneling source of getting people to spend money in your business.

All you must do is start the conversation. For example, I offer special perks to my business neighbors for their employees. Such as waiving the registration fee for 5 or more employees when initiating enrollment. As business owners, when we gain new customers it promotes growth in our business. It may be hard to admit, but at times, you will need help as well. Once you get to know other prominent local businesses, you will discover a wealth of resources and information that can benefit your business.

It is imperative that you build the "trust factor" offline. Who is in your target market? Have you made your self-visible in the Community? Have you planned your business steps?

Download my planner to gain more visibility in your business at

http://childcarebossmarketingandeventplanning.com /monthly.

Bonus: Now we understand why networking is important. This is how to become more involved.

*Join your local Chamber of Commerce and any networking group that may be relevant to your business. Be active and visible for events and dinners within the memberships you participate in.

*Show up at events such as townhalls with local government officials and be visible. Do not be afraid to ask questions and contribute your thoughts and opinions. Your voice will be appreciated and will be remembered by those that are in attendance.

Be active in Business expos and trade shows, both local and abroad. Be ready to hand out your business cards and brochures. Also make sure that if you are unable to host a booth, your brand is well represented through you and your staff wearing branded hats, t-shirts etc.

Challenge: Talk to one business owner in your neighborhood today and ask their name. Exchange business cards and brochures and find one thing you have in common with this business owner besides the neighborhood! Be assertive and don't be afraid to network with your business neighbors.

Mindset of A Mogul

"Once your mindset changes, everything on the outside will change along with it." - Steve Maraboli

As career driven individuals, we all have a desire to achieve success. The drive that we possess begins with our beliefs, passions, attitudes and habits. Normally, there is nothing different that one entrepreneur has that the other in terms of ability. But it does come down to the habits and mindset that encompass commitment and assertiveness towards one's business. A negative attitude can only minimize success and result in a detour towards your success. You must have belief in yourself, knowing that you can achieve anything. It is within this thought process that you will find the power to create the resilience to persevere when adversity appears.

Surround Yourself with Good Company

It is important that you surround yourself with positive and nurturing people as you build your business. Your success depends on it. It only takes one apple to spoil the bunch. It is the same with a toxic person. However, when you surround yourself with other goal – oriented, ambitions, creative and successful people, you can adopt their habits and learn from them as you move towards your goal of success.

No Fear

We were not created to fear. In order to gain success, you must have the ultimate courage and be willing to do courageous acts. You must be willing to go beyond your comfort zone and be willing to encounter the things you are not familiar with. You must know that whether you fail or succeed, you will win from the learning and growth process of the act. When you grow, you have already reached and attained a level of success,

What's Your Vision?

It is important that you have a vision and purpose for your goals. I often write down my goals and aspirations. It is likely that when anything is written down it is achieved rather than staying in one's thoughts. Visualization is powerful because it brings actions to those thoughts and into reality.

Do What You Love

I have realized that in any business, you will more likely succeed if you are passionate about what you do. You must be able to commit to your business, and find purpose in all aspects of your business requirements and duties. How are you benefitting others? There is no other feeling than knowing that you are helping others in your business. When you have love and passion for your business, you will continually nurture it and do what is n necessary to assure that it grows.

Be grateful

As you build your business, there will be good days and bad days. Be thankful for both. Your good days you can relish in, but your bad days are awesome too. Those not so good days will teach you resilience, strengthen your business sense and keep you focused on your goal. Don't allow anything to deter you. Be grateful for everything that is a component of your business growth and success. Keep negativity away from your progress. You must realize how much you have accomplished and how blessed you are in comparison to the situation others may face. It is when you adopt this attitude that you will stop complaining about small matters and come to a place of contentment and joy for what lies ahead for you.

Accept the Challenge

Challenge is an essential part of any type of success in business. Challenge is what creates you into a leader along the journey. You will have challenges with vendors, staff, clients. However, each challenge that causes a barrier in your path, provides you the chance to create a more defined and successful path towards attaining your dream vendors, staff or clients. You must realize that all challenges serve as a way of direction into new opportunities and success in your business overall. Be bold and fearless in your challenges. You must know that you have the power and authority to gain momentum within the challenge. It can only create a better businessperson and prepare you for a higher level of greatness.

Becoming A Mogul

"Invest in seven ventures, yes, in eight; you do not know what disaster may come upon the land."
-Ecclesiastes 11:2

You are ready to start your business. You have found the perfect location. You have the idea for your staff and curriculum. There is a very important component that you can implement that will assist in your overall and future of success of your business. Hire a Childcare/Business Coach. I think it is important that no matter what business you are in that you are open to hiring a mentor to guide you through success in your business. I am a Marketing Coach who specializes in childcare, however, I assist business owners of all genres. During consultations with my clients, I often learn that there are many topics and concepts that they have been ill informed of. When you hire a business coach, you are giving yourself the upper hand in avoiding mistakes and gaining success in your business sooner. I have been blessed with the gift of foresight and creativity which allows me to build solid and lucrative businesses. It is important that you are willing to embrace opportunities to build additional businesses to your childcare. Have you ever heard the saying, "Don't put your eggs in one basket?" One of the greatest downfalls for business owners is becoming comfortable with one stream of income. This can create a disadvantage for yourself as well as your family. It is important to create several streams of income within your business. You may be saying to yourself, "Natalie, I do not know how to create other businesses or market my business." Therefore, you must decide to invest in the future of your business and family by hiring a coach like myself. As entrepreneurs, we must constantly be willing to learn and evolve within our business. I often advise my coaching clients that before you invest a dime, you will need to invest in a coach that can lead you in the right direction. Imagine avoiding mistakes in the progression of your business. There is nothing like possessing a qualified expert to lead you to the path of success in your business. Despite my being a coach, I too have a coach that assists in guiding me into growing my business. I am open to constant learning and I never want my business to be at a standstill. It is wise to hire more than one coach, so you may gain the expertise and perspectives of other Childcare bosses like yourself. Be willing to network and do not be afraid to mingle with those you can learn from.

It is important to promote growth constantly in your business goals. I have been able to assist my clients into creating solid successful businesses that have helped them to create additional businesses. My personal experience is that while building a solid foundation within my childcare business, I was able to springboard into other businesses. I am a Marketing Specialist, Author, CPR and First Aid Instructor and Notary. I have created a conglomerate of businesses that work as one and provides an advantage for the clients I serve. I am constantly open to adding new businesses to my portfolio and willing to seek other opportunities. My business empire continues to expand and I am not afraid to add other streams of income to my business. I am currently the new owner of a makeup and skincare line, *All Mogul,* as well as a Women and Men clothing line, *The Crossover* (mogulfashionllc@yahoo.com), with an exclusive eyewear line.

As a marketing specialist, I incorporate services that will promote my clients to another level and I offer a pathway to success for the novice business owner that will provide assistance that one may not receive from the state.

Unfortunately, the assistance that you will need to promote and accelerate your business will not be provided by your licensing analyst. The State will not assist you in branding or operations, they are only there to regulate. You can avoid violations and exceed the minimum standards enforced by licensing by having a mentor to guide you through the process.

You want to initiate an easier way to succeeding in your business without receiving advise that can lead you to a lengthy and unproductive process. You want an expert on your side. For example, I have a vast expertise in marketing. I have taught owners how to double their enrollment within their centers. I continue to have a waiting list for services. I recently contacted ten prospective students from my center's waiting list to offer enrollment. I enrolled all ten children that were contacted. This is one skill that I teach my marketing and businesses clients.

The life of an entrepreneur is a daily climb to greatness that requires 110% of effort and perseverance. While raising my family, I have been able to contribute to helping other entrepreneurs and their families catapult their lives through successful businesses. I am willing to travel to my clients to assist in achieving their dreams. Location is not a barrier to sharing my expertise with the world.

Entrepreneurship is not an easy road. There is no quick fix to the process, however, there is an easier way that would be beneficial to your business. Many perceive that it is easy and does not take work. On the contrary, it requires sacrifice, determination, focus and the willingness to be open to constantly learning. You are equipped to succeed and win in your business!

Clearly in this chapter, I outline my expertise in business, are you sold? Imagine implementing my marketing strategies with the tools and resources I have towards your success?

If you are interested in learning more about becoming a Childcare Boss Marketing client, contact me @ www.childcarebossmarketingandeventplanning.com.

Remember, in a world full of bosses... be a mogul.

About the Author

Natalie Moore is a multifaceted entrepreneur and mom. Natalie is a native of New Orleans and a survivor of Hurricane Katrina. In her debut work, *Childcare Chronicles*, Natalie provides an account of her pathway from tragedy to triumph in New Orleans. She is the proud owner of a childcare center franchise located in San Antonio, Texas. In addition, Natalie is the owner of *Childcare Boss Marketing* where she operates as a Marketing and Event Consultant to business owners of all genres. Natalie is the proud mother of four and an avid beacon in her local community. Natalie's mission is to assist in transforming the novice business owner into an expert within their field.

"In a world full of Bosses.... Be A Mogul."
- Natalie Moore

Natalie Moore

Childcare Boss, Mentor and Strategist

www.ChildcareBossMarketingAndEventplanning.com

www.FB.com/NatalieMooreChildcareBossMarketing

www.Instagram.com/ChildcareBossMarketing

www.Twitter.com/childcarebossNM

Email: *msnataliej12@yahoo.com*

www.ingramcontent.com/pod-product-compliance
Lightning Source LLC
Chambersburg PA
CBHW070932220526
45468CB00005B/1747